Samuel French Acting Edition

Perp

by Lyle Kessler

SAMUELFRENCH.COM   SAMUELFRENCH.CO.UK

Copyright © 2016 by Lyle Kessler
All Rights Reserved

PERP is fully protected under the copyright laws of the United States of America, the British Commonwealth, including Canada, and all member countries of the Berne Convention for the Protection of Literary and Artistic Works, the Universal Copyright Convention, and/or the World Trade Organization conforming to the Agreement on Trade Related Aspects of Intellectual Property Rights. All rights, including professional and amateur stage productions, recitation, lecturing, public reading, motion picture, radio broadcasting, television and the rights of translation into foreign languages are strictly reserved.

ISBN 978-0-573-70846-6

www.SamuelFrench.com
www.SamuelFrench.co.uk

FOR PRODUCTION ENQUIRIES

UNITED STATES AND CANADA
Info@SamuelFrench.com
1-866-598-8449

UNITED KINGDOM AND EUROPE
Plays@SamuelFrench.co.uk
020-7255-4302

Each title is subject to availability from Samuel French, depending upon country of performance. Please be aware that *PERP* may not be licensed by Samuel French in your territory. Professional and amateur producers should contact the nearest Samuel French office or licensing partner to verify availability.

CAUTION: Professional and amateur producers are hereby warned that *PERP* is subject to a licensing fee. Publication of this play(s) does not imply availability for performance. Both amateurs and professionals considering a production are strongly advised to apply to Samuel French before starting rehearsals, advertising, or booking a theater. A licensing fee must be paid whether the title(s) is presented for charity or gain and whether or not admission is charged. Professional/Stock licensing fees are quoted upon application to Samuel French.

No one shall make any changes in this title(s) for the purpose of production. No part of this book may be reproduced, stored in a retrieval system, or transmitted in any form, by any means, now known or yet to be invented, including mechanical, electronic, photocopying, recording, videotaping, or otherwise, without the prior written permission of the publisher. No one shall upload this title(s), or part of this title(s), to any social media websites.

For all enquiries regarding motion picture, television, and other media rights, please contact Samuel French.

MUSIC USE NOTE

Licensees are solely responsible for obtaining formal written permission from copyright owners to use copyrighted music in the performance of this play and are strongly cautioned to do so. If no such permission is obtained by the licensee, then the licensee must use only original music that the licensee owns and controls. Licensees are solely responsible and liable for all music clearances and shall indemnify the copyright owners of the play(s) and their licensing agent, Samuel French, against any costs, expenses, losses and liabilities arising from the use of music by licensees. Please contact the appropriate music licensing authority in your territory for the rights to any incidental music.

IMPORTANT BILLING AND CREDIT REQUIREMENTS

If you have obtained performance rights to this title, please refer to your licensing agreement for important billing and credit requirements.

PERP had its world premiere in New York City at the TBG Theatre, produced by the Barrow Group Theatre Company (Co-Artistic Directors, Seth Barrish and Lee Brock; Executive Director, Robert Serrell; Director of Production, Porter Pickard), on March 25, 2019. The production was directed by Lee Brock, with scenic design by Edward T. Morris, costume design by Kristin Isola, lighting design by Marika Kent, sound design by Matt Otto, and prop design by Addison Heeren. The production stage manager was Allison Raynes, and the fight choreographer was Ron Piretti. The cast was as follows:

DOUGLASS	Ali Arkane
DETECTIVE HARVEY	Paul Ben-Victor
DETECTIVE JACK	Tricia Alexandro
MYRON	Craig muMs Grant
HARRY	Javier Molina

CHARACTERS

DOUGLASS
DETECTIVE HARVEY
DETECTIVE JACK
MYRON
HARRY

AUTHOR'S NOTES

Detective Jack was originally written for a man, but the character can be played by a man or a woman.

In Scene Four, the Prison Cell was substituted as the Prison Yard. It can be staged in either location.

Scene One

(An interrogation room. **DETECTIVES HARVEY** *and* **JACK** *question* **DOUGLASS**.*)*

HARVEY. Did you do it?
DOUGLASS. Did I do what?
JACK. C'mon.
DOUGLASS. C'mon where?
HARVEY. You know...
DOUGLASS. No.
JACK. ...What we're talking about.
DOUGLASS. I don't know.
HARVEY. Diane...
DOUGLASS. Diane who?
JACK. Diane, tall, blonde, attractive.
HARVEY. A jogger.
JACK. Age thirty-four.
HARVEY. How was she?
DOUGLASS. I don't know how she was. I don't know any Diane.
HARVEY. Did you fuck her before or after you killed her?
DOUGLASS. I didn't fuck no Diane.
JACK. Who did you fuck?
DOUGLASS. I didn't fuck nobody.
JACK. You mean never?
HARVEY. You mean never ever?
JACK. You mean from Time Immemorial?
DOUGLASS. I don't know anything about Time Immemorial.
HARVEY. You're a man.
JACK. You're a grown man.

HARVEY. You don't expect us to believe...

JACK. ...That you never ever...

HARVEY. In all these years...

JACK. ...Fucked a woman.

(Pause.)

DOUGLASS. I fucked a woman.

HARVEY. Good.

JACK. Very good, Douglass.

HARVEY. Now we're getting somewhere.

JACK. We're making headway.

HARVEY. Headway is the Name of the Game.

JACK. One step for man...

HARVEY. ...Kind of thing.

DOUGLASS. It was a long time ago. I was very small. She came to babysit. Her name was Alice.

JACK. Alice, what a bitch, what a deprived person...

HARVEY. ...To take advantage.

JACK. Of a young boy...

HARVEY. Where is she now, this Alice person. Is she alive? Is she dead? Did you kill her? Did you dispose of her body?

DOUGLASS. She's married, she has children, she moved to Arkansas.

HARVEY. It wasn't a question, Douglass. We weren't accusing...

JACK. ...You. We were just testing, we were just probing.

HARVEY. This is what we do.

JACK. We're detectives.

HARVEY. Let me introduce myself. Detective Harvey. And now let me introduce my partner.

JACK. I'd like to introduce myself, Harvey, if you don't mind.

HARVEY. Be my guest.

JACK. Detective Jack.

DOUGLASS. Pleased to meet you.

HARVEY. And we're pleased.

JACK. We're very pleased…

HARVEY. …To make your acquaintance.

> (**HARVEY** and **JACK** *hold out their hands, and* **DOUGLASS** *shakes hands with one and then the other.*)

I'm glad…

JACK. I'm happy…

HARVEY. To get that over with.

JACK. Salutations.

HARVEY. Political correctness.

JACK. Hello, Goodbye, Auf Wiedersehen. Shit like that.

HARVEY. German shit. Gesundheit.

JACK. I prefer American shit, God Bless You.

HARVEY. American shit is so much better than German shit, wouldn't you say, Douglass?

DOUGLASS. Yes, I think so.

HARVEY. Because we're Patriots.

JACK. Say whatever you want of us, but don't take away our love of God, Queen and Country.

HARVEY. Queen?

JACK. So to speak.

HARVEY. I hate "so to speak." I hate that fucking salutation.

JACK. I'm sorry, Harvey.

HARVEY. It hurts, Jack.

JACK. I know it hurts and I'm sorry.

HARVEY. Salutations hurt when taken to an extreme.

JACK. I'm so sorry, it won't happen again. Can we move on?

HARVEY. Yes, let's move on. You see how it is, Douglass, we can get angry.

JACK. We can get upset with each other.

HARVEY. But we make up.

JACK. We get over it.

HARVEY. Because…

JACK. Because we're friends. Would you like to be our friend?

DOUGLASS. Yes, I would like to be your friend. You look like good guys.

JACK. We are good guys.

HARVEY. We are very good guys. We work very hard.

JACK. We have families.

HARVEY. Show him your photos, Jack.

>   (**JACK** *removes a cell phone, shows* **DOUGLASS** *a photo.*)

JACK. These are my boys on their fifth birthday. They're identical twins.

DOUGLASS. They look sweet.

JACK. Well, sometimes.

HARVEY. Ha! Ha! Ha!

JACK. Sometimes they're sweet, other times they're regular devils.

HARVEY. Like most of us, huh, Douglass? Sometimes we can be sweet and other times we can be devils.

JACK. It's called Human Nature.

HARVEY. And you're part of Human Nature, aren't you, Doug? Do you mind if we call you Doug?

DOUGLASS. No, I don't mind.

HARVEY. It's friendly.

JACK. It's less formal than Douglass.

HARVEY. You can call me Harv. And this is Jacko.

JACK. No, not Jacko, it's Jack.

HARVEY. Yes, Jack, I'm sorry, Jack, I apologize.

JACK. Apology noted and accepted.

HARVEY. Fine, good. We were saying, we were discussing Human Nature. And my question to you, Doug is you're not above Human Nature, are you?

DOUGLASS. No, I'm not above Human Nature.

HARVEY. I'm going to show you a photo of Diane now, Doug, okay?

DOUGLASS. Okay.

(**HARVEY** *hands* **DOUGLASS** *a photo.*)

HARVEY. What do you think?
DOUGLASS. She's nice.
HARVEY. Uh-huh.
DOUGLASS. She looks like a nice lady.
JACK. Attractive, wouldn't you say?
DOUGLASS. Yes, attractive.
JACK. Can you be a little more specific? What about her is attractive?
DOUGLASS. She has a nice smile.
JACK. What about her breasts?
DOUGLASS. I don't know her breasts.
JACK. Well, you see her breasts.
DOUGLASS. Yes, I see them.
HARVEY. Do they excite you?
DOUGLASS. I'm not excited.
HARVEY. That's hard to believe.
JACK. I got a hard-on a mile long.
HARVEY. Let's not exaggerate, Jacko.
JACK. I'm exaggerating to make a point. And it's Jack not Jacko.
HARVEY. Excuse me. Jack.
JACK. Pair of breasts like that, Doug. You must've seen them bouncing up and down when she was jogging in the woods.
DOUGLASS. I've never seen this lady.
JACK. You've been to the woods, though, haven't you?
DOUGLASS. Yes, sure I've been to the woods. I walk in the woods all the time.
HARVEY. What do you do in the woods?
DOUGLASS. I collect bugs.
HARVEY. You collect bugs?
DOUGLASS. All kinds of bugs, little bugs, big bugs.
JACK. What do you do with these bugs?

DOUGLASS. I put them into individual little plastic boxes and I study them.

HARVEY. You study the bugs.

DOUGLASS. Uh-huh.

HARVEY. Doing what?

DOUGLASS. Living, eating, breathing, thinking...

JACK. The bugs think?

DOUGLASS. Yes, of course they think. All God's creatures think.

JACK. What do they think, Doug?

DOUGLASS. I don't know their exact thoughts. I just observe them thinking. Take the earthworm for example.

JACK. What about the earthworm.

DOUGLASS. It's a little bug but it's really very significant.

HARVEY. And why is that, Doug?

DOUGLASS. Crawling through the earth, eating the earth, digesting the earth, fertilizing the earth. Millions of earthworms, billions of little earthworms eating, shitting, eating, shitting through China and France, Egypt and Argentina, going about their business in the midst of war and plague and famine. Turning dry and barren land into God's Green Pastures.

*(A faint light illuminates **DOUGLASS** for a brief moment, fades.)*

HARVEY. Can you imagine.

JACK. No, never could, never would.

HARVEY. I just thought today would be one of those days.

JACK. Same ole, same ole...

HARVEY. I'm impressed.

JACK. We are so very impressed.

HARVEY. My mind is swimming...

JACK. At the concept...

HARVEY. Creation!

JACK. Fuckin' Creation!

HARVEY. As exciting as this line of questioning is, I think we should move on.

JACK. That's disappointing.

HARVEY. There are only so many hours.

JACK. Digression sometimes gets you there quicker than a straight line.

HARVEY. That's a profound observation, Jack. If I had pen and paper, I would jot it down.

JACK. Do I detect a hint of sarcasm, Harvey?

HARVEY. God forbid, Jack. I don't have a sarcastic bone in my body.

(Cell phone rings.)

Excuse me.

(Answers it.)

Yeah?

(Pause.)

No, not Pepperoni, Mollie, sausage for Christ Sake.

(Hangs up.)

Jesus!

JACK. I'd like to continue my line of questioning if you don't mind, Harvey.

HARVEY. Sorry.

JACK. You collect bugs in the woods, Doug, and you study them. What about people? You ever come upon any people?

DOUGLASS. Oh, sure, I come upon people all the time. The woods are filled with people.

JACK. Are you interested in people?

DOUGLASS. I'm interested in a lot of things. Bugs, people, current events...

JACK. You're well-rounded.

DOUGLASS. There's a lotta interesting stuff out there.

HARVEY. Did you see Diane jogging?

DOUGLASS. No, never.

JACK. Did you see anyone jogging?

DOUGLASS. Yes, sure, people jog all the time.

HARVEY. And how do you know one of those joggers wasn't Diane?

DOUGLASS. I don't know.

HARVEY. You see, Doug, you see, this is it, you're tripping all over yourself. Tell him, Jack.

JACK. If you were on the witness stand, your ass would be grass because you just perjured yourself.

DOUGLASS. I perjured myself?

JACK. Told a bold-faced lie. Said you've never seen Diane jogging, when in all probability, you've seen her many times.

HARVEY. Diane jogged every day.

JACK. She was into physical fitness.

DOUGLASS. I never thought about it that way.

HARVEY. We're trying to help you here, Doug.

JACK. Give you a kind of Heads-Up so you don't Screw Up.

DOUGLASS. I appreciate that.

HARVEY. We're your friends, Doug.

JACK. We like you.

DOUGLASS. I like you too.

HARVEY. You were in the woods collecting bugs the day Diane was raped and murdered.

JACK. Or murdered and raped. One or the other.

HARVEY. You didn't hear anything strange?

JACK. Anything out of the ordinary...?

DOUGLASS. Nothing.

HARVEY. Not a sound?

JACK. A cry for help?

DOUGLASS. I would have run and helped her if I heard her cry for help.

HARVEY. Because...?

DOUGLASS. Because she was one of God's creatures.

JACK. Like the earthworm.

HARVEY. You have a sterling character, Doug, I can see that.

JACK. For creatures large and small.

HARVEY. You live with your mother?

DOUGLASS. She's a teacher in an elementary school.

HARVEY. So you're on your own a lot.

DOUGLASS. She leaves me a nice lunch every day, and I have the TV and I take my walks in the woods.

JACK. What do you think about this woman being murdered?

DOUGLASS. It's terrible.

HARVEY. Killer used a contraceptive. No way we could collect his DNA.

JACK. Smart fella. How 'bout you, Doug, you use protection?

HARVEY. Or do you go in bareback?

DOUGLASS. I don't go in one way or the other.

JACK. Killer was wearing a black shirt because a piece of it was in her mouth. She had bitten it off in her effort to protect herself.

HARVEY. Do you have a black shirt?

DOUGLASS. I have a lot of shirts.

HARVEY. Do you have a black shirt with a hole in it?

DOUGLASS. No. I have no shirts with holes in them. My mom mends all my shirts.

JACK. You could have thrown it away.

DOUGLASS. I didn't do that.

HARVEY. But if you were the fellow who raped and murdered her you would have thrown it away, wouldn't you?

DOUGLASS. You mean if I was the fellow kind a thing?

JACK. Yeah, sure, if you were the fellow kind of thing.

DOUGLASS. I would probably cut it up with a scissor and flush all the individual pieces down the toilet.

HARVEY. There you go.

JACK. Fantastic.

DOUGLASS. What?

HARVEY. You've entered the mind of the Killer. You know his thoughts, his intensions.

JACK. Not many people can do this.

HARVEY. Very few. A handful. One or two.

JACK. You could be of assistance in this investigation.

HARVEY. There's a Killer on the loose. This is his third victim.

JACK. We can use all the help we can get.

DOUGLASS. I'd like to help.

(Pause.)

JACK. You want to be our friend, don't you, Doug?

DOUGLASS. Yes, sure.

JACK. Hang out with us, chew the fat?

HARVEY. Be one of the boys?

DOUGLASS. Yes.

HARVEY. Do you have any friends?

DOUGLASS. Just the mailman.

JACK. But you only see him for a brief moment each day and never on Sunday.

DOUGLASS. I give him lemonade sometimes. He's always out of breath. He said he has emphysema.

HARVEY. That's not good. That's deadly.

JACK. He won't be around for long. And then you'll be friendless.

HARVEY. I'm going to cut to the chase here, Doug. Would you like to help us solve this crime?

JACK. Bring the killer to justice?

HARVEY. Become a hero.

JACK. In all the papers.

HARVEY. Your picture.

JACK. In the Late-Night News.

DOUGLASS. What do I have to do?

JACK. Confess to the crime.

DOUGLASS. Confess...?

JACK. Yes, it's simple, just say, yes, I did it, I'm the one.

DOUGLASS. And that will bring him to justice?

HARVEY. We throw him a curved ball, make him believe we picked someone else up.

JACK. And then you're convicted.

HARVEY. You're sentenced to life in prison. Case closed.

JACK. Fucking case closed.

DOUGLASS. I don't understand.

HARVEY. That's when the fun begins, Doug. He grows lax, unsuspecting.

JACK. He thinks no one is looking for him anymore. And there we are waiting for him in the woods.

DOUGLASS. You're waiting?

HARVEY. Yeah, we nail his ass.

JACK. His ass is grass.

HARVEY. We set you free and he's convicted.

JACK. The media is all over you. People will stop you on the street.

HARVEY. Ladies will kiss your hand.

JACK. You'll be given the Key to the City.

DOUGLASS. The Key to the City?

HARVEY. We couldn't have done this without you, Doug.

JACK. You are one of us now.

HARVEY. Whaddayuh say, Doug.

JACK. Whaddayuh say, buddy.

HARVEY. You wanna be one of us?

JACK. Join the Party?

>   (**DOUGLASS** *stares in wonder at* **HARVEY** *and* **JACK**, *who smile, expectantly.*)

Scene Two

(A prison cell. A toilet. Bunk beds, one on top of the other. A checkerboard laid out on a wood crate. **MYRON**, *a large African-American man, lies on the bottom bunk.* **DOUGLASS** *stands at the closed cell door holding sheets, a blanket, and a pillow.)*

MYRON. My name's Myron but I ain't a Jew.

DOUGLASS. Oh.

MYRON. You understand?

DOUGLASS. I understand.

MYRON. There's nothing Jewish about me. Do you agree?

DOUGLASS. I agree.

MYRON. You're not just saying so.

DOUGLASS. No, there's nothing about you.

MYRON. Do you know any Jews?

DOUGLASS. I think so.

MYRON. What Jews do you know?

DOUGLASS. I know Sam.

MYRON. Who is Sam?

DOUGLASS. Sam is a Jew.

MYRON. How do you know him?

DOUGLASS. We were in kindergarten together. We lay on mats on the floor next to one another at Nap Time. He invited me to his house. I met his mother and father. I had dinner one time at his house. They said a prayer in Hebrew.

MYRON. Did you join them?

DOUGLASS. Did I join them?

MYRON. In the prayer?

DOUGLASS. No, I don't know Hebrew.

MYRON. Did they try to convert you?

DOUGLASS. No.

MYRON. Did they do any perverted rituals with you?

DOUGLASS. No.

MYRON. They didn't prick your finger and suck your blood?

DOUGLASS. No.

MYRON. And make Matzo out of it.

DOUGLASS. What's Matzo?

MYRON. Unleavened bread, but that's another story. What about your dick? Did they cut off the end of your dick?

DOUGLASS. They didn't touch my dick.

MYRON. Good boy. You don't want anyone anywhere near the vicinity of your dick.

DOUGLASS. I don't intend to let anyone near the vicinity of my dick.

MYRON. Because one thing can lead to another. This is prison if you gather my meaning. My name's Myron. Who're you?

DOUGLASS. Doug.

MYRON. Please to make your acquaintance, Doug. Other fella shared my cell had an accident.

DOUGLASS. What happened.

MYRON. Tripped, broke his neck.

DOUGLASS. That's terrible.

MYRON. Not so bad, was a lousy checker player. You play checkers?

DOUGLASS. Yes.

MYRON. Any good?

DOUGLASS. Pretty good.

MYRON. Other fella was a pushover, no competition. I like competition. I'm all for competition. You beat me at checkers, you're my friend for life.

(He motions to the upper bunk. **DOUGLASS** *begins making the bed.)*

So tell me about that lady you raped and murdered in the woods.

DOUGLASS. You heard about that.

MYRON. It was on the news.

DOUGLASS. What did they say?

MYRON. What could they say. It was a vicious crime. You're a vicious perpetrator.

DOUGLASS. I'm no perpetrator.

MYRON. Oh, no? What are you, Doug?

DOUGLASS. I didn't do it.

MYRON. Yeah, yeah, I know…

DOUGLASS. I mean it, no kidding.

MYRON. We all didn't do what we were suppose to do. I didn't break into a half dozen branches of B of A even though the fella on the Surveillance Camera had an uncanny resemblance to me.

DOUGLASS. They had you on film?

MYRON. They always have you on film. What's this world coming to. Every convenience store, every fucking street corner for Christ Sake. You can't pick your fucking nose without having it immortalized. Big Brother is looking.

DOUGLASS. Big Brother?

MYRON. *1984.*

DOUGLASS. What happened in 1984?

MYRON. The book, not the year.

DOUGLASS. Oh.

MYRON. Listen, you retarded?

DOUGLASS. I don't know what I am.

MYRON. That's okay. I don't know what I am either.

DOUGLASS. Sometimes I have these flashes of incredible insight, other times I don't have a clue.

MYRON. It must be frustrating.

DOUGLASS. Very frustrating.

MYRON. To not be one thing or another.

DOUGLASS. It keeps me up at nights.

MYRON. I imagine.

(Crosses to the checkerboard, sets out the checkers.)

Listen, this is important, this will determine the course of our relationship. Did you rape the woman before or after you killed her.

*(**DOUGLASS** finishes making the bed.)*

Doug?

DOUGLASS. Yes.

MYRON. I'm talking to you.

DOUGLASS. *(Crossing over.)* Could you repeat the question.

MYRON. My pleasure. Did you rape the woman before or after you killed her?

DOUGLASS. I didn't rape no woman.

MYRON. I understand that.

DOUGLASS. I didn't rape or kill no woman. I never killed anyone.

MYRON. Okay, let's come at it from another direction, from a more imaginative direction. If you were to kill a woman, would you rape her before or after the act?

DOUGLASS. I never would kill no woman.

MYRON. I understand that, Doug. This is just a game of What If.

DOUGLASS. What If?

MYRON. Didn't your mom play What If with you?

DOUGLASS. We never played any What If.

MYRON. My mom and I played it all the time. It is what formed my character and made me the fine upstanding individual I am.

DOUGLASS. How does it go?

MYRON. What If…?

DOUGLASS. Yes?

MYRON. …I had all the money in the world, what would be the first thing I'd buy?

DOUGLASS. *(Sits opposite **MYRON**.)* Are you asking me?

MYRON. I'm asking What If...

DOUGLASS. I'd buy a horse.

MYRON. And why is that, Doug?

DOUGLASS. I love horses.

MYRON. You ever ride a horse?

DOUGLASS. I rode a horse once. No, I didn't actually ride the horse, just sat on its back.

MYRON. Go on.

DOUGLASS. I was a little boy and this man came to our house with a pony and a camera and my mom picked me up and put me on the pony and the man took my picture. And that was the happiest moment of my life.

MYRON. Oh...

DOUGLASS. What?

MYRON. That's sad.

DOUGLASS. No, it wasn't sad. I was very happy.

MYRON. Well, anyway, let's get back to the topic at hand. What If. What if you killed that woman, would you rape her before or after?

DOUGLASS. What's the point of raping her after she's dead?

MYRON. There is no fucking point. Only a demented pathologically sick mother fucker would do that, and I don't want to share a cell with any such individual.

DOUGLASS. Neither would I.

MYRON. Well, we are of the same mind. That's a real relief, Doug. I have another question. If you're innocent of this crime, how come you confessed and threw yourself on the mercy of the court?

(Pause.)

DOUGLASS. Can I tell you something?

MYRON. You can tell me anything.

DOUGLASS. I mean in confidence.

MYRON. I won't tell a soul.

DOUGLASS. Cross your heart...?

MYRON. ...And hope to die.

DOUGLASS. I'm here undercover.

MYRON. Is that so?

DOUGLASS. I'm not really a criminal.

MYRON. I could tell that when I first saw you.

DOUGLASS. Detective Harvey and Detective Jack said if I confessed to the crime it would help them catch the real perpetrator who would come out of hiding 'cause he would feel no one was on his tail and he would commit another crime. He would go to prison and I would be released and get the Key to the City and be on the Late-Night News and make a real name for myself.

    (Pause.)

MYRON. They told you that?

DOUGLASS. I would be a hero.

MYRON. The sonsuvbitches.

DOUGLASS. They're nice guys.

MYRON. Listen…

DOUGLASS. What?

MYRON. Let's play some checkers.

    (He makes a move. **DOUGLASS** *studies the board.)*

Scene Three

(The prison cell. **MYRON** *pissing in the bowl, turns, crosses to the bunk.* **DOUGLASS** *reading a magazine on the top bunk.)*

MYRON. This is a Prison.

DOUGLASS. Yes.

MYRON. But it's not really a Prison. It's just a place of incarceration. In the Old Days there were Prisons. I mean real honest to God fuckin' Prisons. Moyamensing Prison. That's an Indian name. Moyamensing.

DOUGLASS. *(Repeating.)* Moyamensing.

MYRON. Conshohocken...

DOUGLASS. Conshohocken...

MYRON. Passyunk...

DOUGLASS. Passyunk...

MYRON. ...The Schuylkill, the fuckin' Schuylkill. Indians fished and swam in the Schuylkill, in the Old Days, in the good Old fuckin' Days. I'm an Indian, did you know that, Doug?

DOUGLASS. No, I didn't know it.

MYRON. I don't look like an Indian, though, do I?

DOUGLASS. No you don't look an Indian, Myron.

MYRON. Appearances can be deceptive. I'm not a full-blown Indian, a half-breed so to speak, not even half but maybe quarter-breed. Maybe not even quarter, maybe even just a drop of Indian blood coursing through my veins. But that teeny-weeny drop of blood is what made me the man I am.

(Pause.)

What made you the man you are, Doug?

DOUGLASS. I don't know, Myron, I have no idea.

MYRON. I can't get over the fact that you beat me.

DOUGLASS. I did my best.

MYRON. No one beats me at checkers.

DOUGLASS. I'm sorry, Myron.

MYRON. No, please don't apologize. I welcome your skill.

(*Crosses to board.*)

Everyone else was a pushover. They offered no resistance. The game was over at the very first move. Now I have something to aspire to. A will to live, to win, to overcome all odds.

(**DOUGLASS** *climbs down from the bunk, crosses over to the checkerboard.*)

DOUGLASS. I'm glad I could be of help.

MYRON. You're filled with surprises, aren't you, Doug.

DOUGLASS. I surprise myself sometimes.

MYRON. So what else do you do for fun, Doug, beside checkers? What do you do for recreation?

DOUGLASS. I collect bugs.

MYRON. Bugs?

DOUGLASS. Yes.

MYRON. What kind of bugs?

DOUGLASS. Any kind of bugs.

MYRON. You don't discriminate.

DOUGLASS. No.

MYRON. Between bugs?

DOUGLASS. No.

MYRON. What about Mankind? Black, white, red, brown races.

DOUGLASS. I don't discriminate between anyone.

MYRON. I could tell. I don't have a prejudice bone in my body myself. What you see is what you get. But that's not the case with you, is it, Doug? What we see is not what we get. You're a fuckin' conundrum, aren't you?

DOUGLASS. I'm no conundrum.

MYRON. Let me ask you this question. Once you come upon a bug, what do you do with the little sucker?

DOUGLASS. Pick it up, study it, observe its behavior.

MYRON. That's wonderful. Really commendable. I've been following your case you know, in the News, on TV, over the Internet.

DOUGLASS. You have?

MYRON. Yes. The fella struck again.

DOUGLASS. What fella?

MYRON. The perp. The man who raped and murdered Diane.

DOUGLASS. He struck again?

MYRON. Once, twice, three times.

DOUGLASS. You're kidding.

MYRON. I kid yuh not. Same fella, same woods, all the earmarks.

DOUGLASS. *(Stands.)* I don't understand...

MYRON. Understand what, Doug?

DOUGLASS. Jack and Harvey haven't called.

MYRON. Well, that's a question.

DOUGLASS. Why haven't they called?

MYRON. That's the same question.

DOUGLASS. They should have called.

MYRON. There are a lotta "shoulds" in this world, Doug. I "should" have been rich, I "should" have been a Sheik with a Harem of beautiful veiled women, I "should" have been in War Paint riding bareback along the Schuylkill.

DOUGLASS. The plan was for me to remain in jail so the Killer would grow lax, unsuspecting, strike again.

MYRON. The Killer has struck again. Not once, but three times.

DOUGLASS. Maybe they've been so busy apprehending him they forgot about me.

MYRON. Maybe, but I would say you are an unforgettable individual, Doug.

DOUGLASS. I appreciate that.

MYRON. I speak from the heart.

DOUGLASS. I bet the papers for my release are being processed this very moment.

MYRON. That would be nice.

DOUGLASS. There's gonna be a knock on the door any second now.

MYRON. And if there is no knock, what then?

DOUGLASS. If there is no knock...?

MYRON. Yes. What do you intend to do?

DOUGLASS. I don't know. I'm not sure.

MYRON. You can sit and wait.

DOUGLASS. *(Sits.)* Yes, I can do that.

MYRON. But for how long? Days, weeks, months, years, forever?

DOUGLASS. I'm not gonna wait forever, Myron.

MYRON. I suspect not. Forever is a long time. Why not strike while the iron is hot.

DOUGLASS. Strike who? I don't wanna strike anyone.

MYRON. Not strike like in hit but strike in like take action.

DOUGLASS. Oh.

MYRON. Understand? Action!

DOUGLASS. Yes, I understand. Action.

MYRON. And so...?

> *(Pause.)*

Doug?

DOUGLASS. I can call them I guess.

MYRON. *Yes!*

DOUGLASS. *I'll call them, Myron!*

> *(He crosses to the cell door, knocks.* **MYRON** *nods, smiles.)*

Scene Four

(**MYRON** *and* **DOUGLASS** *do calisthenics.* **DOUGLASS** *tries to copy* **MYRON**, *has difficulty.* **MYRON** *crosses to the checkerboard, makes a move.*)

MYRON. Your move.

> *(Pause.)*

Your move, Doug.

DOUGLASS. *(Crosses over.)* I can't move.

MYRON. What do you mean, you can't move?

DOUGLASS. I have no more moves.

MYRON. In other words what you're saying is I win?

DOUGLASS. Yes.

MYRON. I'm the winner?

DOUGLASS. Yes.

MYRON. I beat you?

DOUGLASS. You beat me.

MYRON. After how many games?

DOUGLASS. I lost count.

MYRON. I haven't, I've kept a mental record. Two hundred and thirty-two games. I want to go out, I want to go out, Doug and celebrate.

DOUGLASS. I'd like to join you.

MYRON. Go out, pick up some chicks, get drunk, have a ball. Did you ever do that, Doug?

DOUGLASS. No, never.

MYRON. Son of a bitch.

DOUGLASS. I don't mind.

MYRON. But I do, Doug, I fuckin' mind. You know why?

DOUGLASS. Why?

MYRON. Because I like you, I've grown attached to you. I love you, not in a sexual way, God forbid, but in a brotherly way. Do you love me, Doug?

DOUGLASS. Yes, I love you.

MYRON. You're not just saying that.

DOUGLASS. No, Myron, I love you.

MYRON. And why do you love me?

DOUGLASS. Because you're my friend. You care about me.

MYRON. Fuckin' A, Doug. And I've been concerned, because you haven't been your usual self lately, you toss and turn at night and cry out in your sleep.

DOUGLASS. I do?

MYRON. And so I don't know if this is a legitimate win or not because you've been distracted. I wouldn't want to win under adverse circumstances.

DOUGLASS. You won fair and square.

MYRON. A win is a win kind of thing, huh?

DOUGLASS. Yes.

MYRON. I don't buy it, Doug, not even for a second. I reject this win! You weren't up to speed, you were lackluster. There was no get up and go. What's the matter, Doug? What's bothering you?

(Pause.)

DOUGLASS. They haven't responded.

MYRON. Who hasn't responded?

DOUGLASS. Detective Harvey and Detective Jack. I call them each and every day and they are either busy or out of the office.

MYRON. And meanwhile...

DOUGLASS. Meanwhile the Killer has struck again.

MYRON. A fourth time.

DOUGLASS. I don't understand it.

MYRON. I think you do, Doug, I think you do understand it.

DOUGLASS. No I don't.

MYRON. Why are Detective Harvey and Detective Jack avoiding you?

DOUGLASS. I don't know if they are avoiding me.

MYRON. What is it they're doing, Doug? What is the name for it?

DOUGLASS. I don't know the name.

MYRON. They took advantage, Doug. Of your naiveté, of your innocence. They wanted a conviction. They desired a conviction. They didn't give a shit about guilt or innocence, all they cared about is adding another notch to their belt.

DOUGLASS. A notch?

MYRON. A notch, like in the Old West. It's an American custom. Bang, bang, bang you're dead kind of thing. Gunfight at the O.K. Corral. Wyatt Earp, Doc Holliday and the fuckin' Cranston Brothers. A lotta dead Cranstons and a lotta fuckin' notches, one, two, three, four, five notches at least.

DOUGLASS. I can't believe they would do this to me.

MYRON. There are bad people in the world, Doug. There is the Killer.

DOUGLASS. Yes.

MYRON. Who you are not.

DOUGLASS. I am not the Killer.

MYRON. And then there is Detective Harvey and Detective Jack. And they have no love in their hearts, they are even lower than the Killer because the Killer is the Killer, he kills from a compulsion, he is a sick, sick individual who must be stopped but they destroy lives just to get ahead, just to add another notch to their terrible, awful belts.

DOUGLASS. What can I do?

MYRON. I have been put on earth, Doug...

DOUGLASS. Yes.

MYRON. Are you listening?

DOUGLASS. I'm listening.

MYRON. I have been put on earth for this moment.

DOUGLASS. I don't understand.

MYRON. To do a Good Deed. To make amends for all my Bad Deeds. I've been considering this for days, nights. And I know what you need to do.

DOUGLASS. What do I need to do?

MYRON. You need to return to the woods and apprehend the Killer.

DOUGLASS. How will I know it's him?

MYRON. You'll know. You'll recognize him.

DOUGLASS. I will?

MYRON. You know bugs, you know how bugs move and think, you enter the minds of bugs. You can easily enter the mind of the Killer.

DOUGLASS. How can I see him if I'm in prison?

MYRON. Good question.

DOUGLASS. Answer it.

MYRON. You won't be in prison.

DOUGLASS. I won't.

MYRON. You'll be long gone. The Trashman will help you.

DOUGLASS. The Trashman?

MYRON. We both work in sanitation. I will stuff you in a trash can and the Trashman will drive you away.

DOUGLASS. He would do that?

MYRON. He will turn a Blind Eye.

DOUGLASS. A Blind Eye?

MYRON. The Trashman and I have developed a relationship. I shake hands with the Trashman. How many people shake hands with the Trashman, Doug?

DOUGLASS. I don't know. I have no idea.

MYRON. No one, nobody. Outside or inside. Even prisoners look down on him. Hardened criminals, murderers and rapists disdain the Trashman. I love the Trashman, not like I love you, Doug, not like a brother. I love him because he is a fair-minded individual. He cries out against injustice. Trashmen handle the waste products of Society. Broken dolls, ripped and torn clothes, tear-stained love letters, men and women fighting, children crying. The Trashman knows the secrets in each and every house.

MYRON. *(Making it up.)* "Thou shalt know him from what is cast away." Ezekiel, Thirty-six.

DOUGLASS. Ezekiel, Thirty-six?

MYRON. The Trashman will drive you out of the Prison and drop you off in the woods. And then what will you do, Doug?

DOUGLASS. I will wait, I will look, I will, listen.

MYRON. Go on.

DOUGLASS. *I will apprehend the Killer.*

MYRON. Justice will be served.

Scene Five

(Night. **DOUGLASS***, in his prison clothes, sits, holding an earthworm.)*

DOUGLASS. Little bug, little earthworm, crawling through the earth, night and day, day and night, spring, summer, winter, fall...never tired, never weary, crawling blindly on and on fulfilling God's Devine purpose.

(Strokes earthworm.)

Don't be scared, don't be frightened, little earthworm, I mean you no harm. You are the lowest of the low, but you are also the Holy of Holies. You are the mystery we cannot comprehend. God's incomprehensible design for life, for Creation. You are the Chosen One. The Messenger of God. And I hear your message. It's one of love and acceptance. For life, for existence. You do not question. You do not judge. *"Judge not, less ye be judged."*

(He releases the earthworm. A faint light illuminates him.)

Go in Peace, little earthworm, little Child of God.

(The sound of a **MAN** *singing.)*

MAN. *(Offstage.)*
ONE BRIGHT AND SHINING LIGHT
THAT TAUGHT ME WRONG FROM RIGHT
I FOUND IN MY MOTHER'S EYES.

*(***HARRY** *crosses on, a scarf around his neck.)*

HARRY. Hello.

DOUGLASS. Hello.

HARRY. May I join you?

DOUGLASS. Well...

HARRY. I know... I know...you are alone, you are all by your lonesome and you enjoy your lonesome. I can relate to that, I enjoy my lonesome. Who wouldn't...want to get away from people, things, the weight...

DOUGLASS. The weight...?

HARRY. Of the world, crushing down on us. God gave us the woods, didn't he?

DOUGLASS. Yes, he did.

HARRY. To come and relax and enjoy and let our hair down. May I?

DOUGLASS. May you what?

HARRY. Let my hair down.

DOUGLASS. I guess so.

HARRY. Don't be nervous, I don't mean literally let my hair down. I don't have much hair to let down as a matter of fact. It's an expression. It means to relax, enjoy, come clean.

DOUGLASS. Come clean?

HARRY. Another expression. Come clean means be who you are, reveal who you are, be honest and true.

DOUGLASS. I like honest and true.

HARRY. I could tell that the moment I laid eyes on you.

DOUGLASS. Is that true?

HARRY. Would I lie?

DOUGLASS. Well...

HARRY. Ha! Ha! It's just a joke. You don't even know me. But if you knew me you would know that I don't lie, I tell the truth.

DOUGLASS. I tell the truth too.

HARRY. Well, we have something in common. My name is Harry.

DOUGLASS. My name is Doug.

HARRY. I know your name Doug.

DOUGLASS. You know my name?

HARRY. I remember your name from the paper. And your photo. When they apprehended you. All that sturm und drang. Vicious killer. Vicious murderer and rapist of innocent women in the woods.

DOUGLASS. It wasn't me.

HARRY. I know it wasn't you. I'm well aware it wasn't you. Because the murders continued while you were locked away. And then the news that you had escaped. And I wondered why did you have to escape because you weren't the Killer. Why didn't they just open the prison doors and let you walk out.

DOUGLASS. Because Justice doesn't work that way.

HARRY. How does justice work?

DOUGLASS. I don't know, I'm not sure.

HARRY. So here you are.

DOUGLASS. Yes.

HARRY. Hiding out.

DOUGLASS. Yes.

HARRY. An innocent man hiding out in the woods.

DOUGLASS. Yes.

HARRY. And the Police are looking for you.

DOUGLASS. Yes.

HARRY. Because you escaped, you broke the law, you beat the system.

DOUGLASS. I don't know.

HARRY. You took matters into your own hands.

DOUGLASS. I guess I did.

HARRY. I admire you.

DOUGLASS. Thank you.

HARRY. You're my hero.

DOUGLASS. No.

HARRY. Yes. I heard you, Doug. I heard you speak to that little earthworm.

DOUGLASS. You heard me?

HARRY. And I was moved, deeply moved. A man speaking words of endearment to an earthworm.

DOUGLASS. I'm so embarrassed.

HARRY. I would like to know this man, I thought. I would like to be friends with this man. And I don't make friends easily. I live a very solitary existence. What are your plans now that you're free?

DOUGLASS. I have no plans.

HARRY. You must have a plan.

DOUGLASS. Well, I have a plan, one plan, but that's about it.

HARRY. And may I ask what that single solitary plan is.

DOUGLASS. I plan to apprehend the Killer.

HARRY. And how do you expect to do that?

DOUGLASS. I have an instinct.

HARRY. I see.

DOUGLASS. I will know him when I see him.

HARRY. That might be a good instinct but I don't think it would hold up in a Court of Law.

DOUGLASS. Oh.

HARRY. Instincts are not evidence.

DOUGLASS. I never thought of that.

HARRY. Why don't you come home with me.

DOUGLASS. Come home with you?

HARRY. You can't survive in the woods for long. Fall is in the air, winter will come soon, the snow, the frost. I live close by, not far. It's a simple house, no frills, sink, toilet, hot and cold running water and a blow-up mattress in case of company. Do you mind sleeping on a blow-up mattress?

DOUGLASS. I don't mind.

HARRY. And you need to get out of those prison clothes. I have a wardrobe you can choose from.

DOUGLASS. I appreciate that.

HARRY. We are no longer alone, Doug. We are together.

(He holds out his hand, **DOUGLASS** *takes it.* **HARRY** *helps him up. They cross off.)*

Scene Six

*(**DOUGLASS** sits at a small table, eating. **HARRY** serves him out of a large bowl.)*

HARRY. You were hungry.

DOUGLASS. *(Eating.)* Yes.

HARRY. You were starving.

DOUGLASS. No, not starving, hungry.

HARRY. How long has it been?

DOUGLASS. How long has what been?

HARRY. How long has it been since you ate?

DOUGLASS. I don't know, maybe a day or two.

HARRY. Time flies.

DOUGLASS. Yes.

HARRY. When you're having fun.

DOUGLASS. Yes.

HARRY. It's a joke, Doug. Time doesn't fly when you're hiding out all by your lonesome, thinking everyone is against you, the whole world is against you.

DOUGLASS. The whole world isn't against me.

HARRY. Who is for you?

DOUGLASS. Myron is for me. He was my cellmate. And my mom.

HARRY. I stand corrected, Doug, one or two people can make a difference. One or two people can hold back the night. We live in perpetual darkness. It is the good people that cast the light. Do I cast a light, Doug?

DOUGLASS. I don't see a light.

HARRY. Not even a glimmer?

DOUGLASS. *(Staring.)* I don't see any light.

HARRY. This is upsetting. I want to cast a light. I want to be good.

DOUGLASS. Maybe you will be someday.

HARRY. You think so?

DOUGLASS. There's always that hope.

(A faint light shines on DOUGLASS.)

HARRY. You cast a light.

DOUGLASS. I do.

HARRY. Not a bright light, hardly a glimmer. A light nonetheless.

DOUGLASS. I wasn't aware.

HARRY. You wouldn't be. That's the nature of light.

(The light dims, disappears. HARRY picks up the plate.)

How was the food?

DOUGLASS. The food was really good, Harry.

HARRY. Vegetarian chili. Canned. I add some chopped onions and a scoop or two of sour cream. It was my mother's favorite dish. Only she prepared it from scratch. She didn't open up any cans.

DOUGLASS. I didn't mind it canned. I eat canned food all the time.

HARRY. I wish I could do it my mother's way, but I just don't have the time. I miss my mother. I miss her very much.

DOUGLASS. She's dead?

HARRY. She died when I was small. Not small, but small enough.

DOUGLASS. We are all small when it comes to our mothers.

HARRY. I like that, Doug. That was very wise. It resonates.

DOUGLASS. Thank you.

HARRY. What about you, Doug? What about your mother?

DOUGLASS. I miss my mother too. I'm going to visit her when this is all over.

HARRY. Where is she?

DOUGLASS. She is living with her sister in Jacksonville, Florida. She's not well, in fact she's quite sick. She can hardly talk. One word doesn't follow another if you know what I mean.

HARRY. I'm sorry to hear that.

DOUGLASS. I broke her heart.

HARRY. You didn't break her heart, Doug. You were innocent.

DOUGLASS. It broke her heart to see them haul me away to the Police Station.

HARRY. It would break any mother's heart. Mothers are a world apart aren't they, Doug?

DOUGLASS. Yes.

HARRY.
> M IS FOR THE MILLION THINGS SHE GAVE ME,
> O MEANS ONLY THAT SHE'S GROWING OLD,
> T IS FOR THE TEARS SHE SHED TO SAVE ME,
> H IS FOR HER HEART OF PUREST GOLD.

>> *(Pause.)*

> Do you know that song, Doug? Are you familiar with that song?

DOUGLASS. No I'm not, Harry.

HARRY. It's an Old Song. It's a song from a time when there was sentiment in the world. There is no more sentiment. There are no more crooners. The crooners are dead and buried.

DOUGLASS. I'm sorry about that, Harry.

HARRY.
> E IS FOR HER EYES, WITH LOVE-LIGHT SHINING,
> R MEANS RIGHT, AND RIGHT SHE'LL ALWAYS BE,
> PUT THEM ALL TOGETHER, THEY SPELL "MOTHER,"
> A WORD THAT MEANS THE WORLD TO ME.

DOUGLASS. That was lovely.

HARRY. Thank you.

DOUGLASS. Very moving.

HARRY. It brings tears to my eyes whenever I sing it. Would you like to sing it with me, Doug?

DOUGLASS. I would love to, Harry, but I'm afraid I can't.

HARRY. And why is that, Doug?

DOUGLASS. I'm tone-deaf.

HARRY. Who told you that?

DOUGLASS. A teacher in Elementary School. Mrs. Knowy. She said I could stand and sing with the rest of the class in the auditorium but I must only mouth the words.

HARRY. Mouth the words?

DOUGLASS. Pretend I was singing.

HARRY. How could she?!

DOUGLASS. I don't know, Harry.

HARRY. Damage a young man permanently. Make him feel he could never ever sing a song.

DOUGLASS. I sing in the shower.

HARRY. The shower doesn't count. You live in fear and apprehension. You can't even sing in a Karaoke Bar.

DOUGLASS. This is true.

HARRY. *(Twists scarf.)* Where can I find this teacher, Mrs. Knowy?

DOUGLASS. I'm afraid you can't, Harry. She died a long time ago.

HARRY. Fuckin' bitch. Serves her right.

(Motions to **DOUGLASS**.*)*

Stand up, Doug. Stand next to me.

*(***DOUGLASS** *stands, crosses to* **HARRY**, *who places his arm around* **DOUGLASS**'s *shoulder.)*

Now sing along with me.

DOUGLASS. No.

HARRY. Yes, you can do it. Sing with me, Doug.

(He begins singing, **DOUGLASS** *joins him.)*

HARRY & DOUGLASS.
M IS FOR THE MILLION THINGS SHE GAVE ME,
O MEANS ONLY THAT SHE'S GROWING OLD,
T IS FOR THE TEARS SHE SHED TO SAVE ME,
H IS FOR HER HEART OF PUREST GOLD.

HARRY. How was that, Doug?

DOUGLASS. *(Enjoying it.)* It was good.

HARRY. You sang on tune.

DOUGLASS. I did?

HARRY. Yes, we should do more singing,

> *(Hands **DOUGLASS** trousers.)*

Why don't you try this on, Doug, see how it fits.

> *(**DOUGLASS** slips off his prison slacks, puts on the trousers.)*

How do they feel?

DOUGLASS. They feel fine.

> *(**HARRY** hands him a black shirt. **DOUGLASS** studies the shirt.)*

There's a hole in this shirt, Harry.

HARRY. Yes, I know. It adds to its charm.

DOUGLASS. *(Hands it back.)* I'd like one without a hole.

HARRY. What do you have against holes?

DOUGLASS. I have nothing against holes, Harry. In fact I kind of like holes. Take for instance the Black Hole. I heard all 'bout it on the Science Network. All matter, all existence will someday fall into that Hole.

HARRY. That's sick. That's perverted.

DOUGLASS. It's the truth.

HARRY. Then the truth is perverted.

> *(He hands **DOUGLASS** another shirt.)*

DOUGLASS. The truth is the truth, Harry.

> *(He puts on the shirt.)*

HARRY. And what about us? What happens to us when we fall through that hole?

DOUGLASS. We change. We change into something different.

HARRY. Something better or something worse.

DOUGLASS. No one knows.

HARRY. Well, maybe there's hope for me. Maybe the Good become Bad and the Bad become Good.

DOUGLASS. There's that possibility.

HARRY. It's a Crapshoot.

DOUGLASS. All life is.

(He finishes buttoning the shirt.)

HARRY. Whaddayuh think? There are no holes except button holes. Do you have anything against button holes?

DOUGLASS. No, I don't mind button holes.

HARRY. How's it feel?

DOUGLASS. It feels good, Harry, it's fine. Thank you.

HARRY. You've changed, Doug. You have a whole other look to you and you haven't even fallen through some Black Hole.

(Pause.)

That's a joke, Doug. You're not laughing.

DOUGLASS. I didn't realize it was funny.

HARRY. Maybe it's in the delivery. People don't laugh at my jokes, it's a conundrum.

DOUGLASS. A conundrum?

HARRY. The fact of the matter is I don't have much company. Any company to be honest. Not from choice but simply because I don't have the time. There is so much to do and there are not enough hours.

DOUGLASS. Yes.

HARRY. In the day.

DOUGLASS. I wish there were more hours.

HARRY. Can you imagine if there were more hours what we could accomplish. And I don't mean individual man, but Mankind in general.

DOUGLASS. There would be enormous gains.

HARRY. For example the Chinese built the Great Wall of China to keep out the Mongols. They worked day and night for one hundred and fifty years, but by the time they had finished it was too late.

DOUGLASS. Why was it too late, Harry?

HARRY. The Mongols had come through the gaps in the Wall and interbred. They had become Chinese. You can't fight someone if that someone is you, right, Doug?

DOUGLASS. Right.

HARRY. 'Magine if there were more hours in the day. They could have built the Great Wall in a matter of months, weeks.

DOUGLASS. Well, it depends on how many hours.

HARRY. Yes, yes, of course. I'm suggesting a world where there is no restrictions when it comes to hours. Civilization would have advanced at a much more rapid rate.

DOUGLASS. I bet there were no hours in the Garden of Eden.

HARRY. I bet you're right. God isn't into hours. God eschews hours, minutes, seconds…

DOUGLASS. A day could be a thousand years.

HARRY. Man invented hours. Man brought order into Paradise and fucked up everything!

DOUGLASS. Can I help you with the dishes, Harry?

HARRY. Are you changing the subject, Doug?

DOUGLASS. No.

HARRY. I think you are. We were on a roll. We were discussing what was relevant, we were discussing Life Everlasting.

DOUGLASS. We were.

HARRY. Yes, because if you stretched out an hour into infinity, why man would be immortal.

DOUGLASS. I never thought of that.

HARRY. Neither did Einstein. But I did, Doug. Let's stay on target, let's not veer off course. We were discussing mortality.

DOUGLASS. Yes.

HARRY. People die, Doug. This is sad, isn't it?

DOUGLASS. Yes it is.

HARRY. My mother died. I was alone with her in this house, in this room. I was small, not that small, but small enough. I was alone with her corpse. I spoke to her, I said, Mom, Mommy, but she didn't respond. She said nothing.

DOUGLASS. I'm sorry, Harry, I'm so sorry.

HARRY. I prayed to God, but he didn't listen, I don't know if he heard.

DOUGLASS. He heard.

HARRY. You're saying he heard?

DOUGLASS. Yes.

HARRY. How do you know he heard?

DOUGLASS. God hears.

HARRY. Oh.

DOUGLASS. But there's nothing he can do.

HARRY. What kind of a God is it who leaves a little boy alone with the corpse of his mother for days, for weeks, a beautiful, lovely little boy clinging to his mother's rotting, decaying breasts.

DOUGLASS. That's terrible.

HARRY. I was a good boy and I became bad. And I didn't fall through some fucking hole.

DOUGLASS. I'm sorry, Harry.

HARRY. Where were you then, Doug? Why weren't you with me?

DOUGLASS. How could I be with you, Harry. I didn't even know you.

HARRY. You should have been there, Doug. You should have been there.

(Pause.)

Doug?

DOUGLASS. Yes.

HARRY. I'm going to kill you, you know.

DOUGLASS. Yes.

HARRY. Not tomorrow or the day after tomorrow but today.

DOUGLASS. Uh-huh.

HARRY. This hour, this minute, this second.

DOUGLASS. I know, Harry.

HARRY. Whaddayuh mean you know? You don't know.

DOUGLASS. I know.

HARRY. You suspected it when I handed you the black shirt with the hole in it. I did that deliberately.

DOUGLASS. I knew long before then. I knew the very minute and second you appeared.

HARRY. You knew I was the Killer then?

DOUGLASS. Yes. As soon as you said hello.

HARRY. And you came home with me?

DOUGLASS. Yes.

HARRY. You came home with the man who was going to kill you?

DOUGLASS. Yes.

HARRY. I don't believe you. That's crazy, that's insane. Why in the world would you do such a thing?

DOUGLASS. Do you want the short answer or the long answer?

HARRY. I want any answer.

DOUGLASS. I thought I could be of help.

HARRY. And how could you help?

DOUGLASS. If you confessed it might lighten your burden.

HARRY. Ha! Ha! Ha! That's a joke, isn't it. Lighten my fuckin' burden!

DOUGLASS. It's no joke, Harry. Why not try.

HARRY. Okay, I'll give it a whirl. *"I confess, Your Honor. I'm the one, the terrible sick awful psychopath who killed and then raped those women."*

(Pause.)

Doug?

DOUGLASS. Yes.

HARRY. I'm afraid I have bad news. The burden hasn't lightened. The burden still weighs a ton. It's my turn now. I'm gonna lighten your burden. I can strangle you or slit your throat or pour gasoline over your head and set you on fire. What's your pleasure?

DOUGLASS. None of the above.

HARRY. None of the above? That's funny. You're funny. You ever consider Stand-Up?

DOUGLASS. No.

HARRY. It wasn't a real question, Doug, it was rhetorical because there is no time left for you to consider Stand-Up or for anything else for that matter.

(Twists up scarf.)

You gonna choose, or should I choose for you?

DOUGLASS. *(Crosses to him.)* God heard you that day, Harry!

HARRY. *(Confused.)* What day you talking about?

DOUGLASS. The day your mother died and left you all alone.

HARRY. That's not true. God wasn't there!

DOUGLASS. God was right by your side!

HARRY. *Liar! Hypocrite!*
(To the Heavens.) Murderer!

DOUGLASS. God was with you in your suffering but He could do nothing! He was helpless!

HARRY. *(Moving away.) Stop it! Stop what you're doing!*

DOUGLASS. God was in terrible pain.

HARRY. *God?*

DOUGLASS. *Yes.*

HARRY. God was in pain?

DOUGLASS. He was suffering with you in this house, in this room with your dead and decaying mother. A little boy, crying out in pain and God was here with you. Not in actual deed, but in spirit. This is the most we can hope of Him.

(A long pause.)

HARRY. Doug?

DOUGLASS. Yes.

HARRY. I love you.

DOUGLASS. Please.

HARRY. No, it's true. I feel it in my heart. I feel it here. I love you. Do you love me?

DOUGLASS. Yes, of course I love you, Harry.

HARRY. *(Holding scarf.)* How can I kill you if I love you?

DOUGLASS. That's a conundrum.

HARRY. Answer it!

DOUGLASS. I don't know if I can, Harry.

> *(A long pause.)*

HARRY. Doug?

DOUGLASS. Yes.

HARRY. *(Drops scarf.)* I feel a lessening.

DOUGLASS. A lessening?

HARRY. Of the pain, the hurt, the guilt. Do you think he would...?

DOUGLASS. What, Harry?

HARRY. God?

DOUGLASS. Yes?

HARRY. Forgive me.

DOUGLASS. I don't know, Harry. I'm not sure. You can only ask.

HARRY. I can ask?

DOUGLASS. For forgiveness.

> *(**HARRY** stares at **DOUGLASS** a long moment and then bends down on one knee in supplication. A faint light plays over him.)*

Scene Seven

(**DOUGLASS** *stands in a spotlight. A large, oversized key is handed to him. Loud applause.*)

DOUGLASS. I appreciate this Key. The Key to the City of Philadelphia. I never had a key before, any kind of key. No, that's not true. I did have a key once, a tiny little key to my house but I kept losing it and so my mom always left the door unlocked, night and day. She is a very trusting woman, she believes in the Goodness of Man like Anne Frank. I take after her too, I believe in the Goodness of Man, but I also believe in the other side of him. I believe there is Good and there is Evil. And God casts a light upon the Good. And without this light we would be overtaken by darkness and the world we live in would break away from the sun and fall into deep dark space.

(Pause.)

I would like to take this opportunity to say a few words to the Police Commissioner for suspending my sentence and exonerating me. I've never been exonerated before and it feels good. Thank you Commissioner Rhodes.

(Pause.)

I have a confession to make now. A True Confession. I hope you won't think any the less of me but I am nobody's fool. I had a rock in my pocket when I went home with Harry.

(Takes out the rock.)

This very rock. If Harry had attacked me I would have had to defend myself because it is one thing to believe and it is another thing to have Common Sense.

(He pockets the rock.)

I would like to share this key with my mom who is listening and watching in Jacksonville, Florida. Hi,

Mom, love yuh. And I wish to share this key with my friend Myron who showed me the way and without who I would not be standing before you today with the Key to the City but rotting away in some deep dark cell for all my living days which I hope will be many. Thank you Mom and thank you Myron in that order.

Scene Eight

(The Inn of the Slaughtered Lamb. A dark, smoky bar. **DETECTIVES HARVEY** *and* **JACK** *sit drinking. They are a bit unkempt.* **DOUGLASS** *enters.)*

DOUGLASS. Hello.

HARVEY. Doug?

JACK. Fuckin' Doug?

HARVEY. As I live and breathe.

JACK. What a surprise.

DOUGLASS. You called, you asked me to meet you at the Inn of the Slaughtered Lamb.

JACK. We do call, we do inquire, we do entreat.

HARVEY. People come, people don't come, we never know…

JACK. …Who's going to show.

DOUGLASS. Well, I'm here.

HARVEY. Yes, you are and we are honored…

JACK. After all…

HARVEY. You're famous.

JACK. You're a celebrity.

HARVEY. They gave you the Key to the City.

JACK. May we see it?

DOUGLASS. See it?

HARVEY. The Key. We would like to see the Key.

DOUGLASS. I don't have the Key.

JACK. Where is the Key, Doug?

DOUGLASS. It's home, it's at my place.

HARVEY. They gave you the Key to the City and you left it home.

DOUGLASS. It's too big to carry around.

JACK. If they gave me the Key to the City I would have it with me wherever I go.

HARVEY. It's an honor, Doug.

JACK. I would carry it over my shoulder, or let it dangle from my waist. Or have a Chinese Coolie push it along behind me in his rickshaw.

HARVEY. I like that, Jack, that's a nice touch, the Coolie with the rickshaw.

JACK. Because it's the Key to the City, Doug, it's the fuckin' Key to the City!

(Pause.)

DOUGLASS. What do you guys want?

HARVEY. Excuse me?

JACK. I beg your pardon?

DOUGLASS. You called. You asked me to come. What do you want?

HARVEY. Can you believe this?

JACK. I can't believe it.

HARVEY. He's picked up our shit.

JACK. Our shit has rubbed off on him.

HARVEY. Red is white and blue is green in our world.

JACK. We were steering the conversation…

HARVEY. …In one direction.

JACK. And you plunged in and moved it to another.

HARVEY. This is what we do, this is Detective Work.

JACK. Throw the Perp off-balance, by words, by deeds, by changes of expression. This is an expression.

(He makes a funny face.)

HARVEY. *(Makes a grotesque face.)* This is another.

JACK. The perp doesn't know what the fuck is going on. He's pushed one way and then another.

HARVEY. He loses his bearings so to speak. I say, *"Mary had a little lamb."*

JACK. I chime in, *"Mary had a little fuckin' lamb!"*

HARVEY. He's confused, perplexed. He doesn't know how to respond.

JACK. *"Mary had a little fuckin' lamb, mother fucker!"*

HARVEY. *"Speak to me, talk to me, tell me about Mary. And her lamb."*

JACK. *"Her little innocent, never hurt nobody lamb!"*

HARVEY. He's finished, he's gone…

JACK. He doesn't know right from left.

HARVEY. Or up from down.

JACK. He's like putty in our hands.

HARVEY. Just like Harry was putty in yours.

JACK. Fuckin' Harry. Fuckin' killer.

DOUGLASS. Harry wasn't putty.

JACK. What was he, Doug? C'mon! You got your conviction. You nailed the Perp.

HARVEY. And we are so proud of you.

JACK. We knew you had the ability.

HARVEY. But we never imagined…

JACK. …You had the wherewithal.

HARVEY. To size up a situation.

JACK. To risk life and limb.

HARVEY. And go home with the Killer.

JACK. Apprehend the Killer.

HARVEY. In his own lair.

DOUGLASS. It wasn't a lair. It was his home. Harry's not an animal.

HARVEY. What is he, Doug? He's killed and raped.

DOUGLASS. Animals kill when they're hungry. But they have no malice.

HARVEY. I see your point. You're right. Harry's not an animal. Harry's a monster.

JACK. A two-legged walking talking fire-breathing monster. And you caught him.

HARVEY. Can I applaud…?

JACK. May we applaud…

HARVEY. …You?

*(**HARVEY** and **JACK** applaud. A long moment.)*

DOUGLASS. Can I go now?

HARVEY. Can you go now?

JACK. You're asking us if you can go?

DOUGLASS. If you're finished. If you're done with me.

JACK. No, we're not done, we've hardly begun with you.

HARVEY. We asked you here, Doug…

JACK. …Because we are hurt.

HARVEY. Deeply hurt.

JACK. I was more offended than hurt.

HARVEY. Let's not quibble over semantics, Jack.

DOUGLASS. How did I hurt you?

HARVEY. "I would like to share this key with my mom and Myron who showed me the way."

JACK. What about us?

HARVEY. Don't we count?

JACK. We picked you up when you were nothing.

HARVEY. Worse than nothing, nobody.

JACK. Just a thing, a fuckin' thing. And we taught you…

HARVEY. …The Tricks of the Trade.

JACK. How to outwit and maneuver. Dupe and deceive.

HARVEY. And what did we get back?

JACK. Not a word.

HARVEY. Not a token…

JACK. …Of gratitude.

DOUGLASS. Why did you leave me in that Prison?

HARVEY. We didn't leave you in the Prison.

JACK. How could you even think…

HARVEY. …Consider…

JACK. …That we would leave you there.

DOUGLASS. I called and called and you never answered. You never returned my calls.

HARVEY. We were busy. We were working. We were in pursuit of the Killer.

JACK. We had no time to sign papers, print up documents, contact the DA, show him the evidence.

HARVEY. Convince him...

JACK. ...To dismiss the charges.

HARVEY. It would take weeks, months...

JACK. Lives were at stake.

DOUGLASS. I could have helped you.

HARVEY. And you did, Doug. You did help us.

JACK. You apprehended the Killer against all odds and received the Key to the City just like we promised.

HARVEY. You were on the Late-Night News. Women kissed you. Men applauded you.

JACK. Who is applauding Detective Harvey and Detective Jack?

HARVEY. We got left behind in the shuffle.

JACK. There are people who look at us with suspicion.

HARVEY. Who cast aspersions our way.

JACK. People who imply we took advantage of you.

HARVEY. When in fact it was we who showed you the way.

JACK. Who made you the man you are.

DOUGLASS. And what kind of man am I?

JACK. Well, that's a question.

HARVEY. That's to be determined.

JACK. You see, Doug...

HARVEY. Dear Doug...

JACK. There are Killers among us.

HARVEY. You nab one, ten more appear.

JACK. You turn a corner.

HARVEY. There's a Killer.

JACK. You step off a curb.

HARVEY. There's a Killer.

JACK. Doing wrong.

HARVEY. Committing wrongs.

JACK. Wrongs everywhere.

HARVEY. Wrongs falling like rain from Heaven.

JACK. Fuckin' Heaven.

HARVEY. *Fucking God!*
JACK. *Fucking Perp!*

> (**HARVEY** and **JACK** *have pulled out their guns and point them up to Heaven. A long moment.* **HARVEY** *glances at* **DOUGLASS**, *puts his gun away.* **JACK** *does the same.*)

HARVEY. Sorry.
JACK. We're sorry.
HARVEY. We get carried away sometimes.
JACK. At the inequities.
HARVEY. At injustice. The truth of the matter is we need you.
JACK. We want you…
HARVEY. …To help us right these wrongs.
JACK. To twist and turn.
HARVEY. To trick and deceive…
JACK. For a Greater Good.
HARVEY. This is not the Marquis of Queensbury.
JACK. They play dirty, we play even dirtier.
HARVEY. Show him, Jack. Show him the Goodies.

> (**JACK** *hangs a large badge on a chain around* **DOUGLASS**'s *neck.*)

DOUGLASS. What's this?
HARVEY. It's official. We pulled some strings.
JACK. You made the grade.
HARVEY. Detective Doug.

> (*He places a gun in* **DOUGLASS**'s *hand.*)

JACK. Detective fuckin' Douglass. Congratulations.

> (**DOUGLASS** *holds the gun a moment. He places the badge and gun down.*)

DOUGLASS. I don't wanna be a detective.
JACK. You don't want to…?
HARVEY. What do you want?

DOUGLASS. I don't know. I haven't decided. *How many notches?*

JACK. Notches?

DOUGLASS. On your belts.

HARVEY. You mean notches like in the Old West? I like that. How many notches, Jack?

JACK. Who's counting?

HARVEY. More notches than Billy the Kid or Jesse James I imagine.

JACK. But not more notches than God.

HARVEY. The Lord our God. King of Notches.

JACK. Sodom and Gomorrah, the Flood, Plague and Pestilence. We're small potatoes compared with Him. So whaddayuh say, Doug? We three...

HARVEY. Hand in hand.

JACK. Arm in arm...

HARVEY. Righting wrongs.

JACK. Nailing Perps.

DOUGLASS. There are plenty of people out there who would be better at this than me.

HARVEY. Maybe people more educated, but not with your instinct...

JACK. Your incredible instinct and gut nerve...

HARVEY. You're one of a kind, Doug.

JACK. It'll be a feather in our caps...

HARVEY. ...To have you with us.

JACK. It'll remove any doubts of our intentions.

HARVEY. We would have our honor back.

JACK. So whaddayuh say?

(Pause.)

HARVEY. Doug...?

DOUGLASS. How many of the Perps you caught are guilty?

HARVEY. We don't deal with guilt or innocence.

JACK. How could we do our work.

HARVEY. It's up to the Courts to decide.

DOUGLASS. And how have they decided?

HARVEY. In all?

DOUGLASS. Yes.

HARVEY. Tell him, Jack.

JACK. One hundred percent convictions.

DOUGLASS. How can that be?

HARVEY. Because we're dedicated.

JACK. We're relentless.

HARVEY. Nabbing Perps. Prosecuting Perps.

JACK. Prosecutors love us.

HARVEY. Adore us

JACK. Desire us.

HARVEY. Not sexually understand…

JACK. Well, sometimes…

HARVEY. Please, Jack, enough with the hyperbole.

JACK. What about Janet?

HARVEY. How can you even bring up Janet? She fucked the Judge and the Bailiff and most of the Jury. May I finish my point please.

JACK. Yes, please do, Harvey, sorry.

HARVEY. Prosecutors love us because whoever we bring in is convicted.

JACK. A fucking breeze.

HARVEY. A Walk in the Woods.

JACK. So to speak.

DOUGLASS. I'm not interested.

HARVEY. Excuse me.

JACK. Excuse us.

HARVEY. You're not interested?

DOUGLASS. I wouldn't feel good imprisoning innocent people.

HARVEY. I can understand that. I fully appreciate that but no one is truly innocent. I'm not innocent. Are you innocent, Jack?

JACK. No, far from it.
HARVEY. What about you, Doug. Are you innocent?
DOUGLASS. Innocent of what?
HARVEY. Impure thoughts. Rage, anger.
JACK. Unexpressed of course.
HARVEY. Are you so much better than we poor sinners?
JACK. "Who is without sin cast the first stone."
DOUGLASS. I don't know what you're talking about.
HARVEY. You were ready to cast the first stone, weren't you Doug?
JACK. You came prepared.
DOUGLASS. What are you saying?
HARVEY. The rock in your pocket.
JACK. The fucking rock.
DOUGLASS. What about it?
HARVEY. All that talk about Anne Frank.
JACK. And the Goodness of Man.
HARVEY. How long did it take you to select that rock?
DOUGLASS. I don't know. I don't remember.
HARVEY. Minutes, hours…
JACK. Inspecting rocks.
HARVEY. Holding them in your hand, imagining which one was big enough, hard enough, sharp enough…
JACK. …To do lethal damage.
HARVEY. Bash in a head.
JACK. Brains pouring out.
DOUGLASS. I wasn't thinking that.
HARVEY. What were you thinking, Mister Goodness and Light, Mister I can do no Wrong, Mister Better than Us?
JACK. You were going to bash his head in over and over.
DOUGLASS. No!
HARVEY. Yes, you were, Doug. Admit it. It's no crime.
JACK. Guilt, innocence…
HARVEY. It's no crime to kill a Killer.

DOUGLASS. I was just gonna protect myself. I wasn't gonna kill him.

JACK. And if he kept coming at you, this demented Killer, if he didn't stop, if he kept coming, what were you going to do? Split open his head, let the blood and gore spill out?

DOUGLASS. No, no...

HARVEY. Give him the gun, Jack. Let him hold the gun. Let him feel the power.

JACK. The Majesty.

HARVEY. Of the Law.

(JACK holds the gun out to DOUGLASS.)

DOUGLASS. I know what you're doing. I'm not fooling for this. I'm leaving.

(He begins to cross out. HARVEY blocks his way.)

HARVEY. One moment, Doug. We have a gift for you. Show him, Jack.

(JACK places the gun on the table, holds up a metal can, reaches in, and removes a handful of earthworms.)

Earthworms.

JACK. Crawling through the earth, eating, shitting, fertilizing the earth. Little earthworms turning dry and barren land into God's Green Pastures.

(He squeezes the earthworms.)

DOUGLASS. *No! Don't!*

JACK. Fuckin' earthworms!

(He squeezes another handful of earthworms.)

DOUGLASS. *No! No!*

JACK. *(Squeezing.)* Fuckin' precious cocksucking Godforsaken earthworms.

*(**DOUGLASS** picks up the gun.)*

DOUGLASS. *Stop! Stop!*

> (**JACK** *squashes the worms.* **DOUGLASS** *shoots the gun. The revolver clicks. There are no bullets.*)

HARVEY. Gotcha!

JACK. Fucking gotcha!

> (**HARVEY** *punches* **DOUGLASS** *in the face.* **DOUGLASS** *doubles over.*)

HARVEY. Mister Better than Us.

JACK. Mister fuckin' Killer!

> (*He slams* **DOUGLASS** *on his back.* **DOUGLASS** *falls to the floor.*)

HARVEY. Mister Bang Bang you're dead Killer!

> (**HARVEY** *kicking* **DOUGLASS**.)

JACK. Think we'd give you a loaded gun?

HARVEY. We're not crazy. We're not outta our fuckin' minds.

JACK. We're finished with you, Doug. Done. Kaput!

> (*He kicks* **DOUGLASS**.)

HARVEY. Now get outta here!

> (**HARVEY** *and* **JACK** *kicking at* **DOUGLASS** *as he crawls toward the door.*)

JACK. Mister fuckin' Perp!

HARVEY. Mister fuckin' Perpetrating murdering bastard!

> (**DOUGLASS** *crawling,* **HARVEY** *kicking at him.*)

JACK. An' take your miserable earthworms with you!

> (*He throws the remaining earthworms at* **DOUGLASS** *as he crawls through the door.*)
>
> (**HARVEY** *and* **JACK** *give each other high fives.*)
>
> (*Blackout.*)

Scene Nine

(The prison waiting room. **DOUGLASS** *and* **MYRON** *sit across from one another at a table, playing checkers.* **DOUGLASS** *has a bandage on the side of his head.)*

MYRON. I appreciate that you came.

DOUGLASS. Yes

MYRON. In the Old Days...

DOUGLASS. Yes.

MYRON. ...People came.

DOUGLASS. I understand.

MYRON. In the Good Old Days. Friends, relatives. No more though. Time's a bitch, ain't she?

DOUGLASS. I imagine she is.

MYRON. Why do they call her a she rather than a he, Doug? In fact why is Time any gender?

DOUGLASS. I don't know much about gender, Myron. I can't answer that.

MYRON. My Old Man died in prison, did I tell you that?

DOUGLASS. No.

MYRON. Serving Time. Fuckin' Time. And his Old Man before him. It runs in the family.

DOUGLASS. I miss you, Myron.

MYRON. And I miss you, Doug. It's not the same anymore without you.

DOUGLASS. You have a cellmate?

MYRON. Yeah, name a Butch, all arms and legs, not much of a body, face like a mash potato. And an intellect to match. Can't get a word outta him, grunts, groans, shit like that. Forget checkers. Fella wouldn't know the red from the black.

DOUGLASS. I'm sorry, Myron.

MYRON. Nothing to be sorry about, not your fault. We all have our Cross. And what 'bout you, Doug? What happened to you?

(He motions at the bandage.)

DOUGLASS. Detectives Harvey and Jack invited me to the Inn of the Slaughtered Lamb.

MYRON. And you went?

DOUGLASS. Yes.

MYRON. That wasn't a good move, Doug. You know checkers. That was a terrible move.

DOUGLASS. I know checkers all right, Myron. And I will never ever make that move again.

MYRON. Good boy. And how are you otherwise? How you managing?

DOUGLASS. I'm managing okay. I'm working.

MYRON. Doing what?

DOUGLASS. I work for the Trashman. He hired me.

MYRON. No kidding.

DOUGLASS. He took a liking to me. I shook his hand.

MYRON. That'll do the trick.

DOUGLASS. I have dinner at his apartment Mondays and Thursdays. He has a wife and children. He's a Good Man.

MYRON. Yes he is.

DOUGLASS. But I'm not.

MYRON. You're not what?

DOUGLASS. A Good Man. I was a Good Man Once Upon a Time, I'm not good anymore.

MYRON. I don't believe that.

DOUGLASS. I did a Bad Thing, Myron.

MYRON. We all do Bad Things. It comes with the Territory.

DOUGLASS. I could have killed someone. I could have killed Detective Jack.

MYRON. Maybe he deserved it.

DOUGLASS. "Thou shalt not kill."

MYRON. Yeah, I know, thou shalt not do a lotta things, but there are mitigating circumstances.

DOUGLASS. Whaddayuh mean mitigating?

MYRON. And the Lord God said, "There can be no light without darkness."

DOUGLASS. The Lord God said that?

MYRON. It's in the Good Book. Man casts a long shadow. God permits a little leeway.

DOUGLASS. He does?

MYRON. God would never cast his light from you, Doug. *(Making it up.)* "Rejoice Sinner, for he who sinneth against Evil may still enter the Kingdom of Heaven." Leviticus Twenty-three.

DOUGLASS. Is this true, Myron? Does this mean I'm still good?

MYRON. I know from whence I speak.

DOUGLASS. From whence?

MYRON. It's Biblical. From whence, thou shalt, and it came to pass, and so and so beget so and so, shit like that. Biblical shit.

DOUGLASS. Oh.

MYRON. Listen, can we move this game along. I only have a few more minutes

DOUGLASS. I'll be back next week though.

MYRON. I appreciate that.

DOUGLASS. And the week after. I'll be back every week until you get out.

MYRON. If I get out.

DOUGLASS. You'll get out. I know it.

MYRON. If you say so, Doug.

DOUGLASS. I rode my bike along the river yesterday.

MYRON. Uh-huh.

DOUGLASS. The Schuylkill.

MYRON. Oh.

DOUGLASS. And I imagined what it was like in the Old Days, in the Good Old Days, when the Indians pitched their tents along the Schuylkill. And there were Indian families, men, women, girls and boys, fishing and swimming and having a helluva good time. And I heard them laughing, Myron, swear to God, I could hear their laughter. Do you believe me?

MYRON. I believe you, Doug. 'Cause sometimes late at night I hear them laughing.

DOUGLASS. And I thought to myself the very day you get out I'll be waiting and we'll go together to the Schuylkill an' take off our clothes and swim in the river just like the Indians.

MYRON. I hope I get released in the summer then and not the winter.

DOUGLASS. We'll swim no matter what the weather.

MYRON. The Indians never swam in the winter, Doug. The Indians were no fools. They didn't wanna freeze their asses off.

DOUGLASS. I'll bring long johns and wool hats and thick sweaters and a bottle of Jack Daniel's.

MYRON. Jack Daniel's? Now that's a horse of a different color.

(He moves his checker.)

King me.

DOUGLASS. King you?

MYRON. Fuckin' King me, Doug!

DOUGLASS. You're Kinged.

MYRON. And that makes me happy. Even though I probably won't win this game of checkers and even though in all probability I'll never get out of this prison like my father and his father before him, at least I've been Kinged, you understand?

DOUGLASS. I'm not sure.

MYRON. It's the little things in life that have the most significance.

*(**DOUGLASS** stares at him.)*

Your move.

(**DOUGLASS** *studies the board. A light illuminates* **DOUGLASS** *and then* **MYRON**, *at first barely noticeable but then becoming brighter and brighter.* **DOUGLASS** *makes his move.* **MYRON** *studies the board.)*

End of Play

www.ingramcontent.com/pod-product-compliance
Lightning Source LLC
Chambersburg PA
CBHW051411290426
44108CB00015B/2249